D0777711

Introduction

Four and one-half centuries have now passed since the time of the *Brotherly Union*— what has been called the "miracle of the Mennonite church"—which took place in 1527 at Schleitheim, Switzerland. At that crucial meeting, Anabaptist leaders converged upon Schleitheim, worked through fundamental disagreements, and emerged through consensus, with seven points of faith.

The striking immediate and long-range effect of this meeting was an affirmation of faith, couched in simple language which all could understand. The Schleitheim Confession became a powerful testimony that peace as a way of life is the only option for those attempting to live faithfully as the people of God.

Schleitheim functioned for many early Mennonites as a confession of faith, both as a statement of the Christian way of life within brotherhood, as well as a witness and mission to all people. The document was sent out far and wide, inviting its readers to identify with this manifestation of God at work among His people.

The Schleitheim Confession gave substance to

3

a movement which until then had largely been without form, a movement seemingly as varied as the individuals espousing the cause. Schleitheim brought structure and focus.

Mennonites in the 1970s can understand something of the foment of the first two years of the Anabaptist movement which precipitated the Schleitheim Conference. For we have lived through the extremism of the Vietnam era, and we too have emerged battle-worn and scarred. Searching for answers, we have accepted new models originating from a variety of sources, some of them self-contradictory, some of them contrary to the believers' church foundation of gatheredness and peace.

We have tended to gallop off in all directions—and the question still remains: Wherein lies our identity? What, at its very center, is the substance of the current expressions of our real faith? What do we affirm? What do we reject from the multitude of options before us from which we must choose? Wherein lies life's meaning and movement for us who claim to be a small but integral part of God's kingdom?

Most of us know little about the Schleitheim statement of faith, how it came about, and its effect upon the rest of the sixteenth century— indeed its effect upon Mennonites through the centuries. Schleitheim is a valid place to begin, ironic as this may at first appear to some persons wrestling with our current worldwide Mennonite situation.

We would do well to ponder the words of Dale W. Brown, of the Church of the Brethren: "To-

4

day there are signs that some so-called free churches are weary of hearing about the Anabaptist Vision, while it is coming alive in other circles and places. At the same time many folk in the free church tradition continue to acculturate to the main stream, there are others who are discovering with joy the Anabaptist Vision" (*Kingdom, Cross, and Community,* pp. 271, 272).

What faith do we, as a brotherhood-church, confess in common? Although the same 450-year heritage unites us all, many differing answers are heard, even among Mennonites. So it seems appropriate to consider the nature of our heritage, and to note where it differs from the traditions of others who also call themselves Christian. In this process we look for what is true, and also for those elements in our past which have led us away from Jesus and His church.

Perhaps three ideas, central to the Seven Articles of Schleitheim, when taken together, define early Anabaptism: the nature of Christian obedience, the idea of the gathered people of God, and the way of Christian love.

We must tread carefully in considering our past. We no longer live in the rugged sixteenth century when the Anabaptists stood distinctly apart from most Christians in the affirmations just listed. Today Christians from many traditions are accepting the concept of the believers' church; Mennonites too are looking to a broader Christian front in their attempt to be faithful to the call of God. Christian renewal knows no denominational bounds. Our common search and affirmation transcends rigidly drawn traditions and theologies. We have borrowed heavily from other Christian churches; we have given liberally to them from our own deep heritage.

Yet we do want to reflect about our own past. For looking into the past provides us with perspective to face the future God has planned for us.

There is good reason to reexamine Anabaptism as a part of God's work in history, and to come nearer to consensus about faith. Studying the Schleitheim Confession together may well help to bring greater unity to Mennonites today.

—*Leonard Gross*, Executive Secretary
Mennonite Historical Committee
Goshen, Indiana

May 15, 1977

The Schleitheim Confession

Brotherly Union of a Number of Children of God Concerning Seven Articles

The Cover Letter

May joy, peace, mercy from our Father, through the atonement[1] of the blood of Christ Jesus, together with the gift of the Spirit—who is sent by the Father to all believers to [give] strength and consolation and constance in all tribulation until the end, Amen, be with all who love God and all children of light, who are scattered everywhere, wherever they might have been placed[2] by God our Father, wherever they might be gathered in unity of spirit in one God and Father of us all; grace and peace of heart be with you all. Amen.

Beloved brothers and sisters in the Lord; first and primordially we are always concerned for your consolation and the assurance of your conscience (which was sometimes confused), so that you might not always be separated from us as aliens and by right almost completely excluded,[3] but that you might turn to the true implanted members of Christ, who have been armed through patience and the knowledge of self, and thus be again united with us in the power of a godly Christian spirit and zeal for God.

It is manifest with what manifold cunning the devil has turned us aside, so that he might destroy and cast down the work of God, which in us mercifully and graciously has been partially begun. But the true Shepherd of our souls, Christ, who has begun such in us, will direct and teach[4] the same unto the end, to His glory and our salvation, Amen.

Dear brothers and sisters, we who have been assembled in the Lord at Schleitheim on the Randen[5] make known, in points and articles, unto all that love God, that as far as we are concerned, we have been united[6] to stand fast in the Lord as obedient children of God, sons and daughters, who have been and shall be separated from the world in all that we do and leave undone, and (the praise and glory be to God alone) uncontradicted by all the brothers, completely at

8

peace.[7] Herein we have sensed the unity of the Father and of our common Christ as present with us in their Spirit. For the Lord is a Lord of peace and not of quarreling, as Paul indicates.[8] So that you understand at what points this occurred, you should observe and understand [what follows]:

A very great offense has been introduced by some false brothers among us,[9] whereby several have turned away from the faith, thinking to practice and observe the freedom of the Spirit and of Christ. But such have fallen short of the truth and (to their own condemnation)[10] are given over to the lasciviousness and license of the flesh. They have esteemed that faith and love may do and permit everything and that nothing can harm nor condemn them, since they are "believers."

Note well, you members[11] of God in Christ Jesus, that faith in the heavenly Father through Jesus Christ is not thus formed; it produces and brings forth no such things as these false brothers and sisters practice and teach. Guard yourselves and be warned of such people, for they do not serve our Father, but their father, the devil.

But for you it is not so; for they who are Christ's have crucified their flesh with all its lusts and desires.[12] You understand me[13] well, and [know] the brothers whom we mean. Separate yourselves from them, for they are perverted. Pray the Lord that they may have knowledge unto repentance, and for us that we may have constance to persevere along the path we have entered upon, unto the glory of God and of Christ His Son. Amen.[14]

The Seven Articles

The articles we have dealt with, and in which we have been united,[15] are these: baptism, ban, the breaking of bread, separation from abomination, shepherds in the congregation, the sword, the oath.

I. Notice concerning baptism. Baptism shall be given to all those who have been taught repentance and the amendment of life and [who] believe truly that their sins are taken away through Christ, and to all those who desire to walk in the resurrection of Jesus Christ and be buried with Him in death, so that they might rise with Him; to all those who with such an understanding themselves desire and request it from us; hereby is excluded all infant baptism, the greatest and first abomination of the pope. For this you have the reasons and the testimony of the writings and the practice of the apostles.[16] We wish simply yet resolutely and with assurance to hold to the same.

II. We have been united as follows concerning the ban. The ban shall be employed with all those who have given themselves over to the Lord, to walk after [Him][17] in His commandments; those who have been baptized into the one body of Christ, and let themselves be called brothers or sisters, and still somehow slip and fall into error and sin, being inadvertently overtaken.[18] The same [shall] be warned twice privately and the third time be publicly admonished before the entire congregation[19] according to the command of Christ (Mt. 18).[20] But this shall be done according to the ordering of the Spirit of

10

God before the breaking of bread[21] so that we may all in one spirit and in one love break and eat from one bread and drink from one cup.

III. Concerning the breaking of bread, we have become one and agree[22] thus: all those who desire to break the one bread in remembrance of the broken body of Christ and all those who wish to drink of one drink in remembrance of the shed blood of Christ, they must beforehand be united[23] in the one body of Christ, that is the congregation of God, whose head is Christ, and that by baptism. For as Paul indicates,[24] we cannot be partakers at the same time of the table of the Lord and the table of devils. Nor can we at the same time partake and drink of the cup of the Lord and the cup of devils. That is: all those who have fellowship with the dead works of darkness have no part in the light. Thus all who follow the devil and the world, have no part with those who have been called out of the world unto God. All those who lie in evil have no part in the good.

So it shall and must be, that whoever does not share the calling of the one God to one faith, to one baptism, to one spirit, to one body together with all the children of God, may not be made one loaf together with them, as must be true if one wishes truly to break bread according to the command of Christ.[25]

IV. We have been united concerning the separation that shall take place from the evil and the wickedness which the devil has planted in the world, simply in this; that we have no fellowship with them,[26] and do not run with them in the confusion of their abominations. So it is; since all who have not entered into the obedience of faith and have not united themselves with God so that they will to do His will, are a great abomination before God, therefore nothing else can or really will grow or spring forth from them than abominable things. Now there is nothing else in the world and all creation than good or evil, believing and unbelieving, darkness and light, the world and those who are [come] out of the world, God's temple and idols, Christ and Belial, and none will have part with the other.

To us, then, the commandment of the Lord is also obvious, whereby He orders us to be and to become separated from the evil one, and thus He will be our God and we shall be His sons and daughters.[27]

Further, He admonishes us therefore to go out from Babylon and from the earthly Egypt, that we may not be partakers in their torment and suffering, which the Lord will bring upon them.[28]

From all this we should learn that everything which has not been united[29] with our God in Christ is nothing but an abomination which we should shun.[30] By this are meant all popish and repopish[31] works and idolatry,[32] gatherings, church attendance,[33] winehouses, guarantees and commitments of unbelief,[34] and other things of the kind, which the world regards highly, and yet which are carnal or flatly counter to the command of God, after the pattern of all the iniquity which is in the world. From all this we shall be separated and have no part with such, for they are nothing but abominations, which cause us to be hated before our Christ Jesus, who has freed us from the servitude of the flesh and fitted us for the service of God and the Spirit whom He has given us.

Thereby shall also[35] fall away from us the[36] diabolical weapons of violence—such as sword, armor, and the like, and all of their use to protect friends or against enemies—by virtue of the word of Christ: "you shall not resist evil."[37]

V. We have been united as follows concerning shepherds in the church of God. The shepherd in the church shall be a person according to the rule of Paul, [38] fully and completely, who has a good report of those who are outside the faith. The office of such a person shall be to read and exhort and teach, warn, admonish, or ban in the congregation, and properly to preside among the sisters and brothers in prayer, and in the breaking of bread,[39] and in all things to take care of the body of Christ, that it may be built up and developed, so that the name of God might be praised and honored through us, and the mouth of the mocker be stopped.

He shall be supported, wherein he has need, by the congregation which has chosen him, so that he who serves the gospel can also live therefrom, as the Lord has ordered.[40] But should a shepherd do something worthy of reprimand, nothing shall be done with him without the voice of two or three witnesses. If they sin they shall be publicly reprimanded, so that others might fear.[41]

But if the shepherd should be driven away or led to the Lord by the cross,[42] at the same hour another shall be ordained[43] to his place, so that the little folk and the little flock of God may not be destroyed, but be preserved by warning and be consoled.

VI. We have been united as follows concerning the sword. The sword is an ordering of God outside the perfection of Christ. It punishes and kills the wicked, and guards and protects the good. In the law the sword is established[44] over the wicked for punishment and for death, and the secular rulers are established to wield the same.

But within the perfection of Christ only the ban is used for the admonition and exclusion of the one who has sinned, without the death of the flesh,[45] simply the warning and the command to sin no more.

Now many, who do not understand Christ's will for us, will ask: whether a Christian may or should use the sword against the wicked for the protection and defense of the good, or for the sake of love.

The answer is unanimously revealed: Christ teaches and commands us to learn from Him, for He is meek and lowly of heart and thus we shall find rest for our souls.[46] Now Christ says to the woman who was taken in adultery,[47] not that she should be stoned according to the law of His Father (and yet He says, "what the Father commanded me, that I do")[48] but with mercy and forgiveness and the warning to sin no more, says: "Go, sin no more." Exactly thus should we also proceed, according to the rule of the ban.

Second, is asked concerning the sword: whether a Christian shall pass sentence in disputes and strife about worldly matters, such as the unbelievers have with one another. The answer: Christ did not wish to decide or pass judgment between brother and brother concerning inheritance, but refused to do so.[49] So should we also do.

Third, is asked concerning the sword: whether the Christian should be a magistrate if he is chosen thereto. This is answered thus: Christ was to be made king, but He fled and did not discern the ordinance of His Father.[50] Thus we should also do as He did and follow after Him, and we shall not walk in darkness. For He Himself says: "Whoever would come after me, let him deny himself and take up his cross and follow me."[51] He Himself further forbids the violence of the sword when He says: "the princes of this world lord it over them etc., but among you it shall not be so."[52] Further Paul says, "Whom God has foreknown, the same he has also predestined to be conformed to the image of his Son," etc.[53] Peter also says: "Christ has suffered (not ruled) and has left us an example, that you should follow after in his steps."[54]

Lastly one can see in the following points that it does not befit a Christian to be a magistrate: the rule of the government is according to the flesh, that of the Christians according to the Spirit. Their houses and dwelling remain in this world, that of the Christians is in heaven. Their citizenship is in this world, that of the Christians is in heaven.[55] The weapons of their battle and warfare are carnal and only against the flesh, but the weapons of Christians are spiritual, against the fortification of the devil. The worldly are armed with steel and iron, but Christians are armed with the armor of God, with truth, righteousness, peace, faith, salvation, and with the Word of God. In sum: as Christ our Head is minded, so also must be minded the members of the body of Christ through Him, so that there be no division in the body, through which it would be destroyed.[56] Since then Christ is as is written of Him, so must His members also be the same, so that His body may remain whole and unified for its own advancement and upbuilding. For any kingdom which is divided within itself will be destroyed.[57]

VII. We have been united as follows concerning the oath. The oath is a confirmation among those who are quarreling or making promises. In the law it is commanded that it should be done only in the name of God, truthfully and not falsely. Christ, who teaches the perfection of the law, forbids His [followers] all swearing, whether true nor false; neither by heaven nor by earth, neither by Jerusalem nor by our head; and that for the reason which He goes on to give: "For you cannot make one hair white or black." You see, thereby all swearing is forbidden. We cannot perform what is promised in swearing, for we are not able to change the smallest part of ourselves.[58]

Now there are some who do not believe the simple commandment of God and who say, "But God swore by Himself to Abraham, because He was God (as He promised him that He would do good to him and would be his God if he kept His commandments). Why then should I not swear if

I promise something to someone?" The answer: hear what Scripture says: "God, since he wished to prove overabundantly to the heirs of His promise that His will did not change, inserted an oath so that by two immutable things we might have a stronger consolation (for it is impossible that God should lie)".[59] Notice the meaning of the passage: God has the power to do what He forbids you, for everything is possible to Him. God swore an oath to Abraham, Scripture says, in order to prove that His counsel is immutable. That means: no one can withstand and thwart His will; thus He can keep His oath. But we cannot, as Christ said above, hold or perform our oath, therefore we should not swear.

Others say that swearing cannot be forbidden by God in the New Testament when it was commanded in the Old, but that it is forbidden only to swear by heaven, earth, Jerusalem, and our head. Answer: hear the Scripture. He who swears by heaven, swears by God's throne and by Him who sits thereon.[60] Observe: swearing by heaven is forbidden, which is only God's throne; how much more is it forbidden to swear by God Himself. You blind fools, what is greater, the throne or He who sits upon it?

Others say, if it is then wrong to use God for truth, then the apostles Peter and Paul also swore.[61] Answer: Peter and Paul only testify to that which God promised Abraham, whom we long after have received. But when one testifies, one testifies concerning that which is present, whether it be good or evil. Thus Simeon spoke of Christ to Mary and testified: "Behold: this one is

17

ordained for the falling and rising of many in Israel and to be a sign which will be spoken against."[62]

Christ taught us similarly when He says:[63] Your speech shall be yea, yea; and nay, nay; for what is more than that comes of evil. He says, your speech or your word shall be yes and no, so that no one might understand that He had permitted it. Christ is simply yea and nay, and all those who seek Him simply will understand His Word. Amen.[64]

The Cover Letter

Dear Brothers and Sisters in the Lord; these are the articles which some brothers previously had understood wrongly and in a way not conformed to the true meaning. Thereby many weak consciences were confused, whereby the name of God has been grossly slandered, for which reason it was needful that we should be brought to agreement[65] in the Lord, which has come to pass. To God be praise and glory!

Now that you have abundantly understood the will of God as revealed through us at this time, you must fulfill this will, now known, persistently and unswervingly. For you know well what is the reward of the servant who knowingly sins.

Everything which you have done unknowingly and now confess to have done wrongly, is forgiven you, through that believing prayer, which is offered among us in our meeting for all our shortcomings and guilt, through the gracious forgiveness of God and through the blood of Jesus Christ. Amen.

Watch out for all who do not walk in simplicity of divine truth, which has been stated by us in this letter in our meeting, so that everyone might be governed among us by the rule of the ban, and that henceforth the entry of false brothers and sisters among us might be prevented.

Put away from you that which is evil, and the Lord will be your God, and you will be His sons and daughters.[66]

Dear brothers, keep in mind what Paul admonished Titus.[67] He says: "The saving grace of God has appeared to all, and disciplines us, that we should deny ungodliness and worldly lusts, and live circumspect righteous and godly lives in this world; awaiting the same hope and the appearing of the glory of the great God and of our Savior Jesus Christ, who gave himself for us, to redeem us from all unrighteousness and to purify unto himself a people of his own, that would be zealous of good works." Think on this, and exercise yourselves therein, and the Lord of peace will be with you.

May the name of God be forever blessed and greatly praised, Amen. May the Lord give you His peace, Amen.

Done at Schleitheim, St. Matthew's Day,[68] Anno MDXXVII.

Notes

1. A most significant concept in the thought of Michael Sattler is that of *Vereinigung*, which, according to the context, must be translated in many different ways. In the title we render it "Union"; here in the salutation it can most naturally be translated "reconciliation" or "atonement"; later in the text, in the passive participle form, it will mean "to be brought to unity." Thus the same word can be used for the reconciling work of Jesus Christ, for the procedure whereby brothers come to a common mind, for the state of agreement in which they find themselves, and for the document which states the agreement to which they have come. Fast suggests that here, in connection with "the blood of Christ," the meaning might be "fellowship"; cf: 1 Corinthians 10:16.

2. Or, literally, "ordered"; the rendering of J. C. Wenger, "scattered everywhere as it has been ordained of God our Father," is a good paraphrase if "ordained" may be understood without sacramental or predestinarian connotations.

3. This term "aliens" or "foreigners" was interpreted by Cramer *BRN*, 605, note 1, in the geographic or political sense, as referring to non-Swiss. Kiwiet, *Pilgram Marpeck*, Kassel, 1957, p. 44, takes for granted the same meaning and says more sharply that at Schleitheim the Swiss Anabaptists broke communion with the German ones. This understanding is impossible for several reasons:

There was no such strong sense of national identity, divided on clear geographic lines, in the 1520s;

Sattler and Reublin, leaders in the meeting, were not Swiss;

The libertines whom Schleitheim had in mind, although Denck (or Bucer) might have been included, were (if Anabaptist) surely mostly Swiss; namely, the enthusiasts of St. Gall (H. Fast "Die Sonderstellung der Täufer in St. Gallen and Appenzell," *Zwingliana* XI, 1960, pp. 223 ff.), and Ludwig Hätzer.

This term has a quite different reference; it is an allusion to Ephesians 2:12 and 19, testifying to the reconciling effect of the gospel on men who previously had been alienated by unbelief.

4. "Direct" and "teach" have as their object "the same," i.e., the "work of God partially begun in us." Wenger's paraphrase, "direct the same and teach [us]" is smoother but weakens the striking image of a "work of God" within man which can be "partially begun," "cast down," "directed," and "taught." There is, however, ground for Böhmer's conjecture that the original may have read *keren* (guide) rather than *leren* (teach).

5. The "Langer Randen" and the "hoher Randen" are hills overlooking Schleitheim and not, as a modern reader might think, a reference to the fact that Schleitheim is near the (contemporary, political) border.

The original reads "Schlaten am Randen." A good half-dozen villages in southern Germany bear the names Schlat, Schlatt, or Schlatten. One, near Engen in Baden, also is identified as "am Randen," and until recently was held by some to have been the place of origin of the *Seven Articles*. The evidence, now generally accepted, for Schleitheim near Schaffhausen, is easily surveyed:

J. J. Rüger, a Schaffhausen chronicler, writing around 1594, identifies Schleitheim with the *Seven Articles;*

In the local dialect, the equivalent of *ei* in modern German is long *a* as in Schlaten, whereas the other villages Schlatten or Schlat have a short *a;*

Being subject to overlapping jurisdictions and therefore hard to police, the Klettgau, and Schleitheim on its edge, were relatively safe and accessible for Anabaptists and thus a most fitting meeting place linking the major centers in southwest Germany and northeast Switzerland. This was the first area where Sattler's colleague W. Reublin had been active after his expulsion from Zürich early in 1525. This juridical situation continued through the century; Anabaptism was still alive in the Kühtal above Schleitheim as late as Rüger's writing.

Professor F. Blanke reviews the question of place in Z, VI, pp. 104 f.; cf. also Werner Pletscher, "Wo Entstand das Bekenntnis von 1527?" *MGB*, V, 1940, pp. 20 f.

6. According to Böhmer, one line of print was misplaced in imprint A. The text seems to say literally, "we were assembled in points and articles." The verb here is again *"vereinigt."* The "points and articles" may well have stood elsewhere in the sentence in the original text: "we have been united in points and articles" or "to stand fast in the Lord in these points and articles." Wenger's translation, "we are of one mind to abide in the Lord" is the best paraphrase but sacrifices the passive verbal construction which is important to the writer.

7. Beginning with the parenthesis "(the praise and glory be to God alone)," the closing phrases of this paragraph refer not simply to a common determination to be faithful to the Lord, but much more specifically to the actual Schleitheim experience and the sense of unity (*Vereinigung*) which the members had come to in the course of the meeting. "Without contradiction of all the brothers" is the formal description and "completely at peace" is the subjective definition of this sense of Holy Spirit guidance. Zwingli considered the very report that "we have come together" to be the proof of the culpable, sectarian, conspiratorial character of Anabaptism (*Elenchus*, Z, VI, p. 56).

8. First Corinthians 14:33.

9. Ds. H. W. Meihuizen has recently asked with great thoroughness "Who were the 'False Brethren' mentioned in the Schleitheim Articles?" (*MQR, XLI*, 1967, pp. 200 ff.). Meihuizen's method is to survey the entire Reformation scene, Anabaptists of all shadings as well as Reformers, especially those at Strasbourg whom Sattler had recently left. Comparing the known theological positions of these men with the Schleitheim statements, Meihuizen concludes that Schleitheim must have been aimed against Denck, Hubmaier, Hut, Hätzer, Bucer, and Capito. One can agree with this description of the positions in question, without being convinced that the meeting was this clearly directed

against a few particular men who were specifically not invited. If any one person was meant, if would most likely be Hätzer, whom Sattler had just been with in Strasbourg, and who was the only one of these who could be accused of libertinistic leanings. For present purposes, i.e., in order to understand the meaning of this document, it suffices to be clear from the internal evidence (in agreement with Meihuizen):

That some persons previously attached to some of the positions condemned were present at Schleitheim in order to be participants in the event of "being brought to unity"; the "false brothers" referred to by the cover letter were therefore not only state-church Reformers but at least some of them were within Anabaptism:

That the greatest emphasis in the *Seven Articles* themselves falls on those points of ultimate theological separateness from the Reformed: baptism, relation between ban and the supper, sword, oath. Here the list is so parallel to the document from Strasbourg that one surmises that Sattler may have been developing his outline already when he was at Strasbourg;

That in the juxtaposition of the cover letter and the *Seven Articles*, Sattler affirms an inner linkage between the positions of the marginal Anabaptists and Spiritualists who differed from the Zürich-Schleitheim stream, and those of the evangelical Reformers.

10. H. W. Meihuizen reads the phrase "to their own condemnation" as meaning that the Schleitheim assembly took action to excommunicate the libertines whom the text here refers to. "The Concept of Restitution in the Anabaptism of Northwestern Europe," *MQR*, Vol. XLIV, April 1970, p. 149. This is not possible. The verb *ergeben* refers to the libertines' abandoning themselves to lasciviousness, not to the Anabaptists' action. In order to enable this interpretation Meihuizen must omit the parentheses which are in the original.

11. "Glieder" (members) has in German only the meaning related to the image of the body; the overtone of "membership" in a *group*, which makes the phrase "members of God" unusual in modern English, is not present in the original.

12. Galatians 5:24.

13. The use of the first person singular here is the demonstration that the introductory letter was written, probably after the meeting, by an individual.

14. This is the conclusion of the introductory letter and of the epistolary style. The "cover letter" is not in the Bern manuscript, and the *Seven Articles* probably circulated most often without it.

15. With one exception, every article begins with the same use of the word *vereinigt* as a passive participle, which we have rendered thus literally as a reminder of the meaning of *Vereinigung* for Sattler.

16. Here the printed version identifies the following Scripture texts (giving chapter number only): Matthew 28:19; Mark 16:6; Acts 2:38; Acts 8:36; Acts 16:31-33; 19:4.

17. *Nachwandeln*, to walk after, is the nearest approximation in the Schleitheim text to the concept of discipleship (*Nachfolge*) which was later to become especially current among Anabaptists.

18. Two interpretations of this phrase are possible. "To be inadvertently overtaken" might be a description of falling into sin, parallel to the earlier phrase "somehow slip and fall." This would mean that sin is for the Christian disciple partly a matter of ignorance or inattention. Cramer, *BRN*, p. 607, note 2, and Jenny, p. 55, seek to explain that all sin is somehow inadvertent; i.e., that at the time of a sinful decision one is deceived and not fully aware of its gravity. Calvin (with some grounds in the phrasing of the French translation) misunderstood this text to mean that the Anabaptists would distinguish between forgivable and unforgivable sins, with only the inadvertent ones being within the scope of the congregation's reconciling concern. Or the reference may be to the way the guilty person was discovered.

19. The printed version inserts "or banned."

20. This reference to Matthew 18 is the only Scripture reference in the earliest handwritten text. "Rule of Christ" or "Command of Christ" is a standard designation for this text. Cf. J. Yoder: "Binding and Loosing," *Concern* 14, Scottdale, 1967, esp. pp. 15 ff. Other Scripture allusions identified in the footnotes are not labeled in the text. This abundant citation of scriptural language without being

24

concerned to indicate the source of quotation is an indication of the fluency with which Anabaptists thought in biblical vocabulary; it is probably also an indication that they thought of those texts as expressing a meaningful truth rather than as "proof texts."

21. At this point Walter Köhler, the editor of the printed version, suggests the text Matthew 5:23. If "the ordering of the spirit" relates specifically to "before the breaking of bread" and means to point to a Scripture text, this could be a likely one; or 1 Corinthians 11 could also possibly be alluded to; but "ordering of the spirit" is not the usual way in which the Anabaptists refer to a Bible quotation. The phrase can also mean a call for a personal and flexible attitude, guided by the Holy Spirit, in the application of the concern for reconciliation.

22. This is the one point at which the word *vereinigt* is not used at the beginning of an article, presumably because it occurs later in the same sentence.

23. *Vereinigt:* here the word has none of the meanings detailed above, but points to still another; to the work of God in constituting the unity of the Christian church.

24. First Corinthians 10:21. Some texts have here "Saint Paul."

25. Most ecumenical debate about the validity of sacraments focuses upon either the sacramental status of the officiant or the doctrinal understanding of the meaning of the emblems. It should be pointed out that the Anabaptist understanding of close communion refers not to the sacrament but to the participants. It is invalidated not by an unauthorized officiant or an insufficient concept of sacrament, but by the absence of real community among those present.

26. Note the shift from "world" to "they." "The world" is not discussed independently of the people constituting the unregenerate order.

27. Second Corinthians 6:17.

28. Revelation 18:4 ff. Some texts read "which the Lord intends to bring upon them."

29. *Vereinigt.*

30. The printed version adds "and flee."

31. The prefix *wider* can mean either "counter" or "re-"

(modern *wieder-*). Both meanings of course apply to the Reformation churches of Strasbourg and the Swiss cities, which are meant here; they are both anti-popish (having broken with the Roman communion) and re-popish (having retained or reinstated certain characteristics of Catholicism). Earlier translations have chosen the rendering "papist and anti-papist," but the other reading carries a greater pointedness of meaning and is supported by Zwingli's translation. Thus the claim that the new Protestant churches are at some points copies of what was wrong with Catholicism is already taken for granted in early 1527.

32. *Götzendienst*. The Bern manuscript and the early prints read *Gottesdienst* ("worship"); but Zwingli, who had other manuscripts as well, translated "idolatry." Since the next two words both deal with church attendance, "idolatry" is less redundant. "Idolatry" was a current designation in the whole Zwinglian movement for the place of statues and pictures in Catholic worship.

33. *Kilchgang*, literally meaning church attendance, has no congregational dimension to it but refers to the conformity to established patterns of those who, while perhaps sympathizing with the Anabaptists, still avoided any public reproach by regularly being seen at the state church functions.

34. The Bern manuscript reads *Burgschaft*, i.e., a guarantee or security supporting a promise, and belongs in the economic and social realm. If "unbelief" here refers to a lack of sincerity, then the "guarantees and commitments of unbelief" would mean such matters as signing notes and mortgages and affidavits in less than good faith. Martin Luther held strongly that such guarantees, even in good faith, were not only unwise but immoral since the guarantor puts himself in the place of God. ("On Trading and Usury, 1524," in *Works of Martin Luther*, Muhlenburg, Philadelphia, 1931, Vol. IV, pp. 9 ff). His argument is thus very parallel to that of the Anabaptists on the oath. A more likely view is that "unbelief" is synonymous with "worldly," and the reference is rather to guilds and social clubs. Zwingli translates with *foedera*, "covenants." Bullinger bears out this interpretation by reprimanding the Anabaptists at length (*Von dem unverschampten Fräfel. . .* , pp. cxxi to cx-

26

xviii) for their opposition to associations and societies (*pündtnussen und gselschafften*), concord and friendship (*vertrag unnd früntschafft*) with unbelievers, and seemly temporal joy (*zymliche zytliche fröud*). The later printed text changed *Burgshaft* to *Bürgerschaft* (citizenship), which is less in place in Art. IV. In April 1527 Zwingli was unsure what it meant but leaned toward "serving as a guarantor" (Z, IX, p. 112); by August when he wrote the *Elenchus* he interpreted it as "citizenship," perhaps as referring to the Anabaptists' refusal to perform the citizen's oath. But if *Bürgerschaft* should mean citizenship, the "commitments of unbelief" still must mean some kind of involvement, legal, economic, or social, with unbelievers (Z, VI, p. 121). Luke 16.15's reference to "abominations" may be alluded to.

35. The printed version adds "doubtless."

36. The printed version reads "unchristian and."

37. Matthew 5:39.

38. First Timothy 3:7. Interpreters are not clear where the focus of Art. V lies. Its first thrust is a call for the shepherd to be a morally worthy person, i.e., a critique of the practice of his being appointed on the grounds of his education or social connections without regard to moral stature. Zwingli's translation moves the accent by translating "the shepherd should be one from the congregation," i.e., not someone from elsewhere. As Zwingli knew, the Anabaptists also rejected the naming of a minister to a parish by a distant city council, and he let that knowledge influence his translation.

39. The printed version adds, "to lead the brothers and sisters in prayer, to begin to break bread. . . ."

40. First Corinthians 9:14.

41. The change in number here from "a shepherd" to "if they sin" is explained by the fact that this sentence is a quotation from 1 Timothy 5:20.

42. "Cross" is already by this time a very clear cliché or "technical term" designating martyrdom.

43. Perhaps "installed" would be less open to the sacramental misunderstanding. *Verordnet* has no sacramental meaning.

44. "Law" here is a specific reference to the Old Testament. Significantly the verb here is not *verordnet* but merely *geordnet;* conveying even less of a sense of

27

permanence or of specific divine institution. It should be noted that in this entire discussion "sword" refers to the judicial and police powers of the state; there is no reference to war in Art. VI; there had been a brief one in IV.

45. "Without the death of the flesh" is the clear reading of the earliest manuscript. Zwingli, however, understood it "toward the putting to death of the flesh," a possible allusion to 1 Corinthians 5; the difference in the original is only between *a* and *o*.

46. Matthew 11:29.

47. John 8:11.

48. John 8:22.

49. Luke 12:13.

50. Two interpretations are possible for "did not discern the ordering of His Father." This may mean that Jesus did not respect, as being an obligation for Him, the service in the state in the office of king, even though the existence of the state is a divine ordinance. More likely would be the interpretation that Jesus did not evaluate the action of the people wanting to make Him king as having been brought about (ordered) by His Father.

51. Matthew 16:24.

52. Matthew 20:25.

53. Romans 8:30.

54. First Peter 2:21.

55. Philippians 3:20.

56. Here the printed version adds Matthew 12:25: "For every kingdom divided against itself will be destroyed."

57. Matthew 12:25.

58. Matthew 5:34-37.

59. Hebrews 6:7 ff.

60. Matthew 5:35.

61. Zwingli's translation fills in the argument here: "if it is bad to swear, or even to use the Lord's name to confirm the truth, then the apostles Peter and Paul sinned: for they swore."

62. Luke 2:34.

63. The difference in tense between "taught" and "says" is in the original; it results from the fact that Scripture references are always given in the present: "Christ says," "Paul says," "Peter says."

64. This concludes the *Seven Articles*.
65. *Vereinigt.*
66. A second reference to 2 Corinthians 6:17.
67. Titus 2:11-14.
68. February 24.

Literature Relating to the Schleitheim Confession

Augsburger, Myron S. *Pilgrim Aflame*. Herald Press, 1973.

The story of Michael Sattler and the Schleitheim Meeting written in fictionalized form, but based on the historical data.

Bender, Harold S. *The Anabaptist Vision*. Herald Press, 1944 (many reprints).

The classic interpretation of sixteenth-century Anabaptism by a great scholar.

"Brüderlich Vereinigung." *Mennonite Encyclopedia* (hereafter *ME*). Mennonite Publishing House, 1955-59.

An account of the Schleitheim Confession, its background and significance, written by J. C. Wenger.

Burkholder, John Richard, and Redekop, Calvin (eds.), *Kingdom, Cross, and Community: Essays on Mennonite Themes in Honor of Guy F. Hershberger*. Herald Press, 1976.

An attempt to test the winds and discern the Mennonite vision and direction during the 1970s in those areas where disciple meets disciple, and church meets world. A companion volume to the distinguished classic, *The Recovery of the Anabaptist Vision* (see listing below under "Hershberger"), both of which are consciously based upon a common faith and experience.

Friedmann, Robert, "The Schleitheim Confession (1527) and Other Doctrinal Writings of the Swiss Brethren in a Hitherto Unknown Edition," *Mennonite Quarterly Review*, Volume XVI (April 1942), 82-98.

Friedmann was one of the first North American scholars to recognize the true value of the Schleitheim Confession: J. C. Wenger soon followed with an English translation of the Confession three years later (*MQR*, XIX [October 1945], 244-253).

Good, Merle. *These People Mine.* Herald Press, 1973.

Within a handful of beautiful vignettes, the author sketches poetically and dramatically the whole spectrum of Anabaptist and Mennonite history. One vignette is an eloquent testimonial, "The Birth at Schleitheim."

Gospel Herald, February 22, 1977.

A special section on "Schleitheim" prepared in cooperation with the Mennonite Historical Committee.

Hershberger, Guy F. (ed.). *The Recovery of the Anabaptist Vision.* Herald Press, 1957.

This volume contains a strong set of interpretive essays on the historical significance of Anabaptism and the meaning of this movement for the present time.

Martyrs Mirror (edited by Thieleman J. van Braght). Herald Press, 1951.

Contains the story of Michael Sattler (pp. 416-420). Van Braght's inclusion of the Sattler story in this Dutch work would suggest some influence of Sattler—and of the Schleitheim Confession—upon Low Country Mennonitism. (Indeed, the Schleitheim Confession was translated and published into the Dutch language in 1560, and again in 1565 another clue to the significance of the Schleitheim Confession for Dutch and North German Mennonitism. See above, "Brüderlich Vereinigung," for this documentation.)

"Sattler, Michael." *ME*.

This lengthy account is a moving story of the life and significance of Sattler for the development of the Anabaptist-Mennonite movement.

"Schleitheim." *ME*.

This essay presents the background material to the meeting itself of those who created what later would become known as the Schleitheim Confession.

Wenger, J.C. *Conrad Grebel's Programmatic Letters of 1524*. Herald Press, 1974.

Here is the first synthesis of Anabaptist thought, containing the kernel ideas of what later would be incorporated into the Schleitheim Confession.

Yoder, John H. *The Legacy of Michael Sattler*. Herald Press, 1973.

Contains excellent background information to the Schleitheim Confession, which places this most important Confession in its historical and theological setting (see especially pp. 27-34 and 47-48 for an appraisal of how the Schleitheim Confession has been interpreted historically and theologically over the centuries). Also includes other writings of the significant Anabaptist thinker and martyr, Michael Sattler. The volume is central in understanding the idea and setting of the Mennonite faith.